Thurber Tower

Thurber Tower

The First Year of the Rest of My Life

Gay Hadley

with illustrations by Dave Weltner

Bryan Books

Bryan Books

645 Neil Avenue, Suite 418
Columbus, Ohio 43215

Design · Jenna Dixon · djinna.com
Text composed in Bembo

All events and characters in this book are based on real
people and situations. They are mostly factual except for the
author's occasional forays into silliness. Names have been
changed, except for Ellie West with permission from her family.

ISBN 978-0-9904061-3-6

Printed in the United States of America

14 15 16 17 18   6 5 4 3 2

This journal is dedicated to my
Thurber friend Ellie West
who lived to the very end of her life.

Contents

GROUP TOURS –

Foreword

Life is a series of new beginnings. New residents of Thurber Tower, an independent living residence in Columbus, Ohio, redirect their energy to new life patterns and Gay Hadley has done just that in the last year.

After eight decades of life in Columbus, Gay moved to Thurber Tower in 2012. Among her many activities, Gay is a writer—and life in Thurber Tower offered abundant inspiration. This book collects her writings from Year One as she explored life in her new home.

Gay Hadley's creative writings allow you to explore the world of living in a senior community. Brace yourself, parts of this new world may surprise you!

Thank you, Gay, for capturing the essence of life here at Thurber Tower.

—Joel Wrobbel

Joel Wrobbel is the director of marketing at Westminister-Thurber Community where Thurber Tower is the residence for independent living. He is also host of the Ohio radio progam Journey Through Aging (journeythroughaging.org). Westminster-Thurber Community, established in 1965, believes in serving the whole person and creating opportunities for each individual to live life their own way through providing a myriad of choices through its ongoing programs and services.

Thurber Tower

Letter to Myself

Am I becoming completely unhinged; making a gracious and generous decision for my family's sake; or starting another adventure? This is one of many mental exercises I undertake each day while I whittle down a lifetime of possessions in preparation for my move to a retirement center.

A retirement center? Ten years ago, when I turned seventy-two, I was convinced that a retirement center was not in my future. I had put a shower in the downstairs bathroom, installed two closets in the laundry room and purchased a trundle bed for the living room alcove. I was set for the rest of my life. I could live downstairs, keep the upstairs for family and friends, and then hire a graduate student to live with me when I needed more consistent, in-house help. How clever of me to anticipate everything!

All of that before I turned eighty, then eighty-one and then . . . one of those almost imperceptible shifts began to make going out at night by myself a major undertaking. The wrought-iron fence around my front yard began to turn brown and cry out for my attention and maintaining my tiny garden was no longer fun. Against this backdrop of decreasing zeal for home ownership and its attendant responsibilities, an unexpected and unsought offer to buy my house appeared out of the blue and served as the impetus to explore (oh no!) a retirement community!

This time, living with engaged and engaging elders near at hand, having a snowplow and exercise facilities standing by and an in-house library to lounge in appeared deliciously inviting. How could this have happened without my anticipating it, without my considering changes beyond the one I had planned for? Thirty years earlier, as an administrator in Human Resources at The Ohio State University, I had designed and facilitated a retirement planning workshop/course for faculty and staff! Taught by a gerontologist, a lawyer and a financial planner, with me picking up a few topics like housing and lifestyle issues, the course was, for its time and for a university, something of a novelty.

Now here I am . . . hoisted by my own petard . . . caught short by unanticipated life changes . . . wondering why I never noticed! As I pack for this move and wander in a dazed fashion among multiple piles for multiple relatives, I find myself reminded (again) about the pitfalls of certainty at any age!

Apartment #714

from my balcony I see
the university rising
at the edges of a world
I have chosen
for the rest of my life
parameters drawn by age
by pride about being able
to take care of myself
not to be a burden
on children who would
call it something else
and be there anyway
so much for boundaries
as for horizons . . .
great books, fresh ideas,
the public square, old friends
and newer ones ready to be
known and gently tended,
unforeseen serendipities
Lord, let me stay alive
to what is in waiting

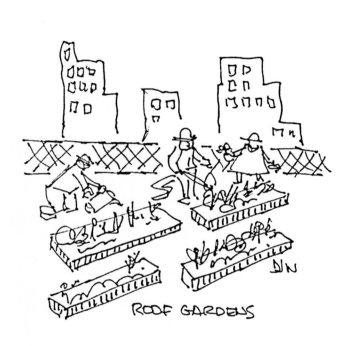

ROOF GARDENS

Ages and Stages

Back in the 1920s, when many of us who live in Thurber Tower were born, the research of the French psychologist Piaget began to produce a new paradigm for childhood, an emerging understanding of our first years as not only a separate stage of life but also a stage that could be broken down into clear, age-based steps in cognitive development.

Although our own childhoods were not greatly affected by the findings of Piaget and others, we certainly raised our children with full knowledge of what babies and children could be expected to know and do at each age and stage along the way. So influential and pervasive were the effects of this research that we parents could work ourselves into a tizzy if our children did not measure up to what the charts had to say about age-appropriate behavior. Having a son about three whose only word was "motorcycle" led us to the pediatrician who assured us his vocabulary would grow before he went to college!

Again, as our generation moved into its middle years, researchers were also beginning to identify adulthood as a separate, identifiable stage of life with its own characteristics and its own clear developmental markers. The popularizer of adult development theory was Gail Sheehy, who gained fame and fortune with her book, *Passages*, which was published in 1971. Do you remember? Were you as excited as I was to find that adults could, and in many cases did, meet major life events with new and expanded options, beliefs and behaviors? Although Sheehy was accused of simply popularizing the work of academic researchers, it was she who brought the understanding of adult development to the mainstream.

Like never before, more adults went back to school; changed careers in mid-life, developed entirely new interests and hobbies and made contributions in fields previously dominated mostly by the young. We who now live at Thurber were, in many ways, beneficiaries of the expanded opportunities for middle-aged and older adults.

And what about the present, now that we find ourselves in a group called "the elderly"?

After all, there are four decades of us living at Thurber Tower! We range in age from our 70s to 80s to 90s and over 100! The oldest group is, of course, the fastest growing. How long can we still be lumped together as one group? And, is it only our physical health and our cognitive capacities that differentiate us? Or are we profoundly changed, not only by our individual adult histories but also by the events in the public sphere that affected our own particular age group, for example, the depression, World War II, assassinations, civil rights and women's movements, as well as television, computers, and the web. Already we can see distinctions between the pre-computer elders and those of us who use computers. How do both the private and the public events of our adult years impact our aging?

Although our health in general and our cognitive capacities are the two most frequently-cited differences within the group called elderly, could we imagine that with the arrival of the zillions of boomers into this category, we might begin to differentiate between and among us even more, partly because our differences as well as our numbers will affect many areas of public policy including retirement planning? These are things I (age 83) think about from my perch in Thurber Tower, things I thought about when I was in my forties and things our children and grandchildren will have to think about as they age differently into entirely different worlds.

Tell me, is this exciting or not?

Point of View

I used to see
a sea of gray and white
swell in slow motion,
ebb and tide.
Living here I see
a multitude of faces
etched by lives lived large
each one a book for opening,
each day a new creation
to bank against the cold.

Ed Brown

Ed Brown is a quiet man. Mostly, he sits in the lobby on the far edges of any and all conversations, his base-ball cap tipped toward the back of his head, his gnarled hands placed peacefully in his lap and his demeanor edging on something akin to quiet resignation or sad-ness. Or so I had thought, until one day he reached out and thrust into my hand a periodical called *The Progressive*! I was doubly surprised, not only by Ed's lefty leanings but also by the fact that a tacit agreement seemed to prevail at Thurber Tower that politics would be discussed on a selective basis, an acknowledgment that if you are going to live with people in close quar-ters, it is wise to refrain from potentially inflammatory subjects. The front lobby, being a place where almost everybody appears at one time or other, was perhaps an unwise choice of place for a political discussion.

Yet, what could I do? The overture had been made, the gauntlet thrown down. So I pulled a chair up close to this intriguing "old man" and was immediately pulled into his spell. His liberal leanings, he told me, came from his father who was a miner and therefore a union man. (If you were a miner in southeastern Ohio or West Virginia when Franklin Delano Roos-evelt ruled the country, you were a Democrat, at least if you knew which side your bread was buttered on!)

Moving from Gallipolis (famous for the Silver Bridge disaster), down to Bellefontaine, East Liverpool, Martins Ferry (home of Ohio poet James Wright), and St. Clairesville, Ed's intimate knowledge of these southeastern towns, hollows and hills revealed him as a curious man. He vividly described the loss of farmlands that sent people into the mines for a living and into the cultivation of marijuana and meth instead of golden seal and black cohash. Then, of course, came the closing of the mines which sent young men like Ed to the cities for work.

Whether it was glassmaking in Toledo, tires in Akron, perch in Lake Erie or Ford cars in Lorain, Ed could tell you pretty much anything a person would want to know about Ohio's geography, fish and wildlife, or manufacturing. He is, as he himself said, an American historian.

Old in the Act of Becoming

A certain softness sets in.
Bones no longer
sit up straight.
Our skin takes on
a camouflage.
Errant thoughts take off
without our bidding
and we fail to hear
essential things
like birds or rain
or multiplying years,
the sum of which
do not reveal
who we are, who
we might yet be.

first published in *Porcelain Dreams*, 2010

SHUFFLEBOARD

Charlie Turner

The Westminster-Thurber shuffleboard team has built a fine reputation as one of the best teams in the league. Boarding the W-T bus at the early morning hour of seven, the members travel to retirement communities all over Ohio to eat breakfast, compete, have lunch and return to Thurber by five. Their maroon knit shirts with Westminster-Thurber stitched above the pocket identify them as a team to be reckoned with. In addition to the players, a small entourage of supporters goes along on the team's trips in order to cheer the players on, provide comfort in the event of a loss, and enjoy two good meals and a bus trip.

Charlie Turner learned to play the game on a carrier ship in World War II and he has retained his love for it throughout his life. Charlie would never tell you that he was the best player on the team but word has it that his scores were almost always the highest ones to be reported. And Charlie learned more than shuffleboard during the war. He learned French.

His skill was put to use for women in the Thurber Tower elevator who were deemed by Charlie to be particularly susceptible or charming. Any woman stepping into the lobby from the elevator with a slightly alarmed expression and with Charlie trailing behind could be presumed to understand enough

French to be either amused or slightly embarrassed. Collecting the mail at the huge bank of mailboxes was a special treat if Charlie happened to be getting his at the same time. His sibilant cooing could make a girl blush and drop her letters at Charlie's feet (or so the story was told).

Oh, Charlie! Where were you when I was young?

Attention Extroverts

The bulletin board that hangs opposite our mailboxes is enough to give an introvert pause. On any given day, one might read:

- Four notices about shuffleboard practice and scheduled contests
- Six bus routes to grocery stores and shopping centers
- Sign-up sheets for the Columbus Symphony, Ballet Met, the Columbus Clippers and the Central Ohio Quilt exhibit
- Balance classes and aerobics schedules
- Reminders of dates for Book Club, current affairs Friday morning group, art classes and the knit and crochet group
- A recipe for the cheese dip someone brought to hospitality hour

And, in case one does not read the bulletin board, another relentless schedule of activities is enclosed in our weekly paper, *The Chatterbox*, which is slipped under our doors every Saturday morning.

In the face of what might seem to be a frightening level of hyperactivity, introverts need not despair. We can hide out indefinitely in our own apartments,

the local park, bars, libraries, or in the basement somewhere. Thurber Tower is home to an impressive number of musicians and writers and shy people who have
lived long enough to know their druthers and insist
upon their privacy. At least, I think we do . . . you will
excuse me while I go to aerobics.

Hazel Morris

Hazel Morris is a woman of habit. She sits in one of the mustard yellow armchairs that grace the front lounge of her independent living complex. That is, she sits there four hours each day. From 9 to 11 every morning and from 2 to 4 every afternoon. This punctilious habit allows Hazel to observe the comings and goings of the majority of the residents of her apartment building. In addition, because Hazel lives in a one-bedroom on the first floor, she almost always notices when the squad arrives and whether or not the squad leaves with anyone in tow, blanketed and therefore partially disguised from curious onlookers.

Hazel is the one constant in the lobby gatherings of residents who sit there for a visit at one time or another during the day. Generally speaking, the conversation centers on the life of the retirement community—who has moved to assisted living, who is waiting for a larger apartment, how the new herb garden is faring, and what new restaurants have appeared in the neighborhood. A couple of suspected liberals do huddle in the corner occasionally to share editorials from the *New York Times*. And movie buffs always report their latest cinema finds.

For Hazel, the highlight of the day occurs when any of the dogs who live at Thurber pass through the lobby on their way out. No dog is admitted to Thurber who weighs more than 24 pounds so the variety of pooches is limited. Among Hazel's favorites are a wire-haired terrier named Sport who is beautifully groomed and who holds his aristocratic head high at all times. Then there is Mabel, a refugee from Katrina, who is barrel-shaped and mild-mannered. Maddy, who is Hazel's favorite, has the head and tail of a shi-tzu and the body of a poodle. Since she is mostly white except for a large black spot on her back, she resembles a Rorschach test to some of the more academic residents.

Hazel keeps a cache of small and medium-sized dog biscuits in the pocket of her blue cardigan and the dogs have come to expect a treat from her in return for a modest amount of petting. After months of daily treats, Maddy agreed to jump into Hazel's lap and succumb to her extended massages. This amicable friendship developed into a daily ritual that brought enormous pleasure to both parties as well as to Maddy's owner who came to entrust Hazel to hold the dog's leash while she (the owner) ran one or more brief errands. It was such a successful Share-a-Dog plan that other owners began to ask other lounge sitters to hold their pooches' leases while they also did errands or ran the sweeper or took walks at a rather more vigorous pace than their dogs would ordinarily allow.

It became a not unusual sight to step out of the elevator and be confronted with an equal number of dogs and people sitting in the lobby. And Hazel, who started all this, found herself quite pleased to have initiated the ritual. Having been more of a follower than a leader all of her life, Hazel enjoyed the attention that came her way. It even reminded her of her first husband, Harry, who also liked a good snuggle now and then.

One day, the director of Thurber Tower (a kind of housemother with the patience of Job and problem-solver with the wisdom of Solomon), stopped to chat in the lobby with our canine assembly. She suggested we might want to form a club for the owners and their surrogates, a gathering where we might discuss the shared problems and joys of dog ownership/surrogacy in a highrise for senior citizens. In spite of a plethora of other groups, committees, and volunteer opportunities designed to keep us busy in the event that we did not already know how to do that, there was an enthusiastic response from the dog crowd.

Thus it was that another discussion group was born in Thurber Tower; another slate of officers proposed; another meeting schedule developed. And Hazel, who had never been elected president of anything, came into her own as the presiding officer. Her only stipulation: the meetings must end by four so she could start fixing her dinner.

Taking Comfort

Old Cat and I curl
in a patch of winter sun.
Me, beneath a quilt
of yellow poppies.
She, snug in her
calico coat.
We like being old
and dreamy
when no one else
has time, when the sun
departs before the day
can stretch
to its full length.

first published in *Porcelain Dreams*, 2010

Copier Machine Supervisor

In the roster of positions for the Thurber Tower Residents Association Board is one that caught my eye. There, I thought, is a job that would suit me. No committees required; the work could be completed on my own time and I would be free, then, to pursue my own interests without feeling like an escapee from the world of civic responsibility. So when asked, I said yes. Surely, with the help of another more gadget-minded resident, I could keep the thing going, faithfully collect the change twice a week and turn it over to the treasurer. Not as high-minded as the Library Committee Chair or as clearly philanthropic as the Visit the Ill contingent, the task had to be done and somebody had to do it.

Taking on this mantle of modest responsibility made me feel I was ending my career at approximately the same level as I began it in the second grade by taking milk orders, collecting the money, and slipping into the hall to deliver my order to the cafeteria. Thus we begin to collect our transferable skills which should, according to the experts, be banked for future use in the job market. Career counseling guru, Richard Bolles, author of the all-time best-selling *What Color Is Your Parachute,* maintains that a job is "the way you put your skills together to do meaningful work."

It is to him that I owe my success in putting together my volunteers skills in a way that helped me begin a paid career in the middle of my life. Somehow, in the process, Copier Machine Supervisor never showed up on a list of jobs that matched my skills and experience. An oversight, no doubt.

From Bolles' perspective (and mine), Copier Manager is just as honorable work as any other. Provided, I would add, if you can find a way to also use your "higher" skills. That being said, I would read books, try to write and engage in long, lazy conversations with enlightening friends . . . a reasonable career plan when you are eighty-three. It seems to me that Thurber residents have an extraordinary willingness to take on any work that needs to be done, from watering plants to cooking eggs for patients in the Nursing Unit. After all, we helped run the world once! We do not have to do that any more.

Ellie West

I first met Ellie over a glass of wine in my new apartment. A mutual friend had put us in touch. But it was Ellie herself who told me during our long, engaging conversation that she was living with stage-four cancer. She wanted me to know that she had every intention of going full-steam ahead in spite of the fact that chemo days "could be trying."

Ellie kind of snuck up on people. Her low, calming voice and demeanor were misleading indicators of a multi-talented woman with brains and guts. Although she wore fashionable black-rimmed glasses like Meryl Streep's as fashion editor in *The Devil Wears Prada*, Ellie's comportment otherwise appeared to be more like a Mrs. Dalloway.

Belying her calm demeanor and following the trajectory of many privileged 1950s women, Ellie went back to school, earned her CPA, went into business with her husband, and developed her quilting skills to the level of an accomplished artist. Then, quietly, as it so often goes, her roseate life began to take on darker hues. Having already placed their oldest child in a home for special-needs kids, one-by-one they watched their three boys marry and migrate. Not long after, Ellie's husband died and she herself became critically ill. So, in her intentional and organized fashion, she stitched herself together and moved to Columbus to be near her sons and their families.

And, importantly, to continue her life as artist in her small apartment where she had a made-to-order closet built to accommodate the tools of her trade. Hanging on wooden dowels that run from the top to the floor of each closet wall are bolts and bolts of exquisite materials. The fabrics took my breath away as did the quilt she was working on, a collage of brilliant colors being stitched on a black background, a metaphor, or so it seemed to me, for her life and times.

So this, her family and her art, is what will keep her going, what will make it possible for her to live to the very end of her life.

Going on Eighty

Like a child who longs to be ten
says she is ten
from the day she turns nine,
I have been going on eighty for years.
It is my four-minute mile, my blue ribbon
for persistence if not skill.
Enough, I say, eighty will be enough.
Still, I had a dream
about a craggy place, a stone's throw
from a mountain peak
from where you could, if you stood on
your toes and peered over,
see a felicitous land
you have never visited
that looks exactly like home.

first published in *Porcelain Dreams*, 2010

The Flip Side

Retirement communities can scarcely be accused of false advertising based on a failure to list one of their most salient characteristics: the inevitable presence of dying and death. Quite to the contrary, I find that living with the everyday realities of death has turned out to be one of the richest of all the daily changes from living in my own home.

Take the simple "ritual of the flippers." All the apartment doors in our tower of independent residents is equipped with a little piece of wood, shaped like an exclamation mark, swinging on some kind of screw in the door frames. Every night, a staff member goes to all ten floors and flips every flipper up. Every morning a resident volunteer on each floor checks all the doors to make sure the flippers are down, indicating the door has been opened. One can see why this routine is not used as a selling point for the community!

Yet I find these simple flippers reassuring and the phone call from the desk if I have failed to open the door a comforting reminder that someone really is watching over me. The proof of the pudding, so to speak, occurred a few months ago after I had been working with another resident on one of her very complex and difficult word puzzles (we were stumped by a ten–letter name for a tennis star who had won the majors a prodigious number of times!). In the course of these encounters, I had come to admire this understated, highly accomplished, and frail woman who was keeping the machinery of her mind well lubricated.

The next morning, her flipper was up and when the staff member went to check on her, it was clear she had died in the night. The manner of her passing was greeted with a real sense of relief for her and an agreement that this was the way to go. Hers was the first service of memory in the W–T chapel that I attended and I sat beside a woman who had lived here fourteen years. "These services get harder the longer you live here," she said. As indeed they would.

"Doesn't all the death make you sad?" This question is almost always asked by one of the ever-so-young nursing students who come on a quarterly basis to talk informally with a panel of residents. Yes, we reply, but it also makes each day more precious. The ever-present reality of loss seasons our days with a poignant immediacy.

Class Reunion

No hint,
> her silver hair,
> indigo roped hands,
> lavender muslim loose
>> where a waist would be,
>> where the spine begins
>>> its lazy curve.

No hint,
> until her voice
> (a cadence recalled),
> and her laughter
>> spilling
>> across the lawn,
>>> lapping me up.

Elizabeth!
> I knew you would come!

first published as "Reunion Class of 1937" in *Porcelain Dreams,* 2010

RED, WHITE AND BOOM
ON THE ROOF

Self-Governance

The balance in a retirement community between its professional staff and the residents is a delicate one. I can think of no more difficult position than that of administrators in places filled with former executives, school principals, professors, judges, elected officials, and presidents of The League of Women Voters! "You mean *you* are going to tell *me* when the dining room is open, the kind of trees that will be planted outside my window, where I have to put my recyclables!"

The fact is that most retirement community residents do assume some governing responsibilities in the form of Resident Associations replete with officers and regular meetings. We begin with the Pledge of Allegiance (group singing optional) and continue with reports from the officers and committee heads. Current committees include Transportation, Grounds, Library, Employee Recognition, Cubby Corner, and OWLS (Older Wiser Learners). We make up more committees as the perceived need arises which it frequently does.

But the highlight of these meetings is the real director's* report which must provide a satisfactory

*The director, "Grand Poobah," is the chief administrator of Westminster-Thurber Community.

summation of the entire communities' activities and current challenges with clarity, authority, and humor. Then the meeting is opened for resident remarks, many of which are complaints in the guise of questions and questions in the guise of statements. It disturbs me, I remark to a friend, that more people do not express appreciation for something . . . anything, in fact. They do, my friend says, but not in the meeting. I hope she is right. We, the people (I have heard) includes directors . . . so thank you! All of us are grateful.

What It Comes Down To

a short story

Mary Alice is eighty-three years old and still remembers every detail of her cheerleading outfit. That is because her happiest times remained her junior and senior years in high school. Nothing, absolutely nothing, including college, marriage, motherhood, or being secretary of the PTA trumped the wonder of being a cheerleader in high school, of being seen by parents and players alike making happy under the lights. Some people might call Mary Alice's trajectory of joy a case of arrested development. Others, who remember the fifties, the suburbs and Dwight Eisenhower as the apotheosis of the American dream will understand her fixation.

Two years after high school, Mary Alice hit a hard bump in the road. She dropped out of the local community college and married a gorgeous young man who proved, after quickly producing two children, that he had no staying power, no interest in monogamy or earning a living or anything else that might tie him down. So it was that Mary Alice, at the age of twenty-one, found herself in a dim apartment with two babies and no idea of what to do next. Her fall from grace was epitomized for her by the gold sweater with a block

N on the front and her black pleat-around, wool twill skirt that hung in the back of her meagre closet. She could not even bear to look at the black and white saddle shoes resting on the closet shelf high above her head.

With prodding from her parents, Mary Alice found a job as a glorified filing clerk in a prestigious law firm. Her mother came every day to watch the children and life took on a hue of dependability and monotony. Mary Alice's happiest times were the monthly lunches she shared with high school friends. Their conversations began, and sometimes ended, with a running commentary about "whatever happened to . . ." and their get-togethers continued without interruption well into their dotage.

The toddlers Mary Alice was so proud of turned three and four before the rhythms of her life began to shift. At last, an eligible man presented himself. Not just any man but a young lawyer who worked in the firm where Mary Alice filed away her days. Harold was, to put it charitably, not a very handsome man who was disposed to peering over his horn rimmed glasses as if he was about to pounce on you in court with a series of horrifying accusations. That aside, he dressed meticulously and he was so excessively polite to all the clerks and secretaries it appeared almost unseemly.

It was with mixed feelings that Mary Alice accepted Harold's invitation to dinner and while she did not particularly enjoy her date, she very much enjoyed going out for an expensive meal, being seated by the maitre d' and being seen by two of her friends and their husbands. You can guess where this is going and that is where it went. In spite of the fact that Harold was a Roman Catholic and Mary Alice a divorced

Presbyterian, he was willing to get married by the County Clerk of Courts and hope for a conversion later. Harold accepted the little ones with an encouraging degree of equanimity and, after a honeymoon in the Keys, the four of them settled into a sweet story-and-a-half in the suburbs.

After three years, Mary Alice and Harold had added two more children to the mix, another boy and another girl which made for a symmetry pleasing to their parents. And the marriage progressed rather nicely, all things considered. Harold had his own den where he read the Wall Street Journal, did his taxes, worked the daily crossword, and let the children in at seven or so every evening to say goodnight. Mary Alice mothered so well that Harold was surprised when the oldest child left for college.

You might ask if this was a happy marriage. Both Mary Alice and Harold would probably say that it was. Each got their primary needs met and neither of them longed for things they could not have. The central staying power was Mary Alice's conversion to Catholicism after the Bishop figured a way around the fact that she was a divorcee. St. Andrews became a grounding place for both the parents and the kids who were baptized and catechized and ultimately married with the complete approval of everyone who needed to approve.

When Harold retired, his constant presence at home put a crimp in Mary Alice's social life. And Harold, who had always wanted to go to exotic places like Singapore or Bhutan was frustrated that he could not talk his wife into anything more than Myrtle Beach or visiting the children. In spite of these minor adjustments for both of them, the years passed in mutual equanimity until Harold began to grow steadily more irritable and disconsolate. It was something Mary Alice had not observed before. It was unsettling that he would not even disagree with her, would not go to Krogers or the wine store, and even stopped reading the sports pages. Clearly, this was more than an aberration so she insisted on a doctor's appointment. And that is when Harold was diagnosed with Alzheimer's (the early stages) and was sent away with little more than a stack of pamphlets. Mary Alice drove Harold home, settled him in his chair, and went to the kitchen to fix lunch.

Two years slipped by as Harold grew more and more reclusive, gave up his *Wall Street Journal,* and stopped watching football. The days passed peacefully for him. He seemed content to stare out the window although Mary Alice was never quite sure what he saw. The changes in his life patterns were much more difficult for Mary Alice, or so it seemed to her. She gave up her lunchtimes with friends, her shopping trips with her daughters, and the church's couples group they had attended for forty years. But she still went to the beauty parlor once a week to have her lovely white hair washed and set while a daughter watched Harold. She also went to see a priest who prayed for Harold.

Harold's death at the age of eighty-one was not entirely unwelcome. Everyone said he was out of his misery and no doubt quite happy about where he found himself. The children and grandchildren all stayed after Harold's funeral service and burial. They shared a potluck supper with Mary Alice. Then they did the dishes and went home.

Mary Alice, not knowing what to do, went to her closet, climbed her stepladder and retrieved her black and white saddle shoes. She put them on and sat down in Harold's chair where she fell asleep.

Three years later, Mary Alice moved to an apartment on the fourth floor of an independent-living highrise called Thurber Tower on the edge of downtown Columbus. She liked seeing the lights of the city at night. They made her feel that she had come a long, long way.

Jane McDonough

One might expect to see a face like hers when tramping the fells in England's Lake District or in the Scottish Highlands. This face, replete with freckles, an enquiring expression, parsimonious mouth and brown eyes that dance behind her glasses is the face of a bright, opinionated and highly educated woman. And that she is. Jane McDonough, now with cane instead of walking stick, in a retirement community instead of on a college campus, is still blessed with a mind that percolates with opinions she holds with fervor.

Something about her says that she does not suffer fools gladly which made me feel quite happy to engage with her initially in a discussion about books we were reading. The book she loaned me, *Ordinary Wolves*, a tough-minded novel about wolves in Alaska and about people scavenging perilous lives in the wilderness, suggests a wide ranging literary sensibility. One would need to scramble in order to keep pace with this insatiable reader.

Jane is not given to passing time by exchanging social pleasantries. Rather she heads, with her book, to the Bistro and to one particular reclining chair which gives her back some ease while she reads. There she spends a couple hours each afternoon before she takes an early supper in one of the dining rooms. Her other, and as far as I can tell, favorite times are spent with her daughter who is a psychology professor at Ohio State, a daughter who also possesses a prodigious mind.

These two forged an unbreakable bond as single mother and child in the fifties, a decade before the feminist gains of the sixties even began to make the difficult path for professional women somewhat smoother. Makeshift work for Jane led to a leadership career in the Girl Scouts; a return to college, a Ph.D. in psychology at the University of Minnesota; and a distinguished academic record at Iowa State. Little wonder that Jane's daughter chose the same discipline for her own academic pursuits!

I think sometimes there is no way that younger women of any age can fully appreciate the courage and endurance of women who forged wider educational and career opportunities for them. The least we can do is salute them . . . and I do.

This I Believe

Children are the main reason for hanging around.

People who go on learning also go on living.

Eating alone is hard without a book.
The best meals are seasoned
        with great conversation.

Pursuing differences is more rewarding
than maintaining sameness.

Living life fully takes a lot of courage.

Nothing is more beautiful than pear trees
in April, more delicious
        than Ohio sweet corn in August.

I would rather live as if there is God than
as if there is not.

Poetry gives life grace. Friends give it joy.
Family keeps it rooted.

    . . . life ends when the mind stops beating.

The Great Unspoken

Heads, shoulders, knees and toes, knees and toes . . . The nursery rhyme we played as children in the 1930s has long since become the subtext for the body parts that we can now speak about. Born long before the pill when sex prior to marriage was scandalous, as elders in a retirement community we now live as if sex is still a subject not open to discussion.

When the human potential movement was at its peak in the sixties and some of us were joyously participating in workshops and "encounters," one entrepreneurial psychologist was making hay out of helping adults to admit and deal with their "skin hunger," a term which might well be revived among the elderly today.

My observations, here in Thurber Tower, lead me to believe that in public . . .

> older women hug, briefly and seldom;
> older men do not.

The result suggests that most elders are skin hungry. How many of us would admit this is quite another question. So physical affection in public spaces remains mostly taboo. If I am incorrect, will somebody come forward and tell me?

- PHYSICAL FITNESS -

Dave Walton

Dave Walton is not a creation of Horatio Alger. While he did grow up poor in the Bottoms during the Depression, he did not jump off a speeding train or rescue a damsel in distress from a burning building. Nor did he become a rich and famous English Lord! What he did do was create a successful, happy and enormously creative life by being the artistic, people-loving and genuine person he was born to be.

Born in 1927, Dave helped support the family by selling newspapers, an early forecast of his life's work. He was an average student with two passionate interests, drawing and music. He learned to play the trumpet in junior high and went on playing it for sixty years in marching bands, jazz groups, and wherever he could find willing partners. Now that his air-power is no longer up to a trumpet, he plays the harmonica literally all over town. In the summer, you will find a foot-stomping crowd at Johnson's Ice Cream on Main Street where Dave will be playing the blues with the Bexley Jam Band.

It was the love of drawing and his pursuit of that love that led Dave to a lifelong career, most of it with the Columbus Dispatch. After two years in the Army as part of the Japanese occupation and a brief stint at Ohio State, he enrolled in the Central Academy of Commercial Art in Cincinnati where he learned to be a graphic designer. He returned to Columbus where his first job was with a plumbing manufacturer. Drawing toilets and other plumbing fixtures, however, is the only thing that Dave was unable to be enthusiastic about. In 1951, he jumped at the chance to go to work for the Columbus Dispatch. And therein hangs the tale of a successful career and a passionate loyalty to the Wolfe family, owners of the Dispatch, WBNS, and other enterprises.

Dave is a textbook case of a one company man who rose into top management by taking on every new opportunity and learning while he went: from artist to Copy and Layout; then Sales where he serviced large accounts like Bill Owens Appliances, Rite Rug, and Sun TV; another series of promotions starting with Assistant to the Assistant Retail Manager and ending up as Retail Manager. And, finally, into the ranks of top management as Ad Director. Dave learned as he went. Since he did not know one end of a budget from another, he taught himself at night. He is amused that when he retired, the job description to replace him required an MBA!

Dave married his beloved Barbara in 1956. By mutual agreement, she stayed home, supported him all the way, and raised their two children. And Barbara, from a small town (Jackson, Ohio), had her own learning curve as Dave's career required more and more hobnobbing with the rich and famous, including many a fancy affair at the Wigwam, the Wolfe family's showplace.

Dave was gone from home a great deal. He networked with business executives across the country

and found himself belonging to almost every downtown organization. But this expanding professional
career did not change Dave and Barbara's values one
bit. Although they lived well and traveled the world,
Dave maintains to this day that he still has "boundaries in my mind I cannot break." His loyalty to the
Wolfe family is part of what is unbreakable.

Barbara and Dave stayed in Gahanna which was
their home and they did not succumb, as Dave says,
to "the acquisitive life-style." A 56-year membership
in the Mifflin Presbyterian Church, a founding member and designer of the Gahanna Community The-
atre, and a widely published political cartoonist, Dave
spread his talents in many directions.

Heart surgery in 2000, followed by Barbara's incip-
ient illness led them to Thurber Tower where Dave
cared for his wife until she died. He moved to a one-
bedroom apartment where he would not live every
day with memories. And guess what? He goes on
playing his harmonica, seeing his boodles of friends,
and walking out the door with a jaunt that says "here
is a happy man."

Our Daily Bread

This is not an advertisement! It is a simple fact of life in a church-owned retirement community that religious activities suffuse our daily life. A chapel stands near the center of the complex of buildings. A full-time chaplain is present in every sense of that word. A group of residents offers a rich menu of services and programs. On Sundays, the flow of residents going to churches is a steady one. Carpools to St. Frances and a bus to a Methodist church swell the outgoing traffic.

Muslims, Jews, non-believers, and separation-of-church-from-other-activities advocates should know that *nobody* but *nobody* will encroach on your own belief or non-belief at Thurber Tower! I think that I would, if I could, sit in a lotus position wrapped in gauze for eight hours and, although some might stare (for good reason), none would intrude or deny me that right . . . no, you try it!

If faith is love made evident, my first year at Thurber has been filled with thoughtful gestures and, yes, acts of love. A meal at my door, a vase of flowers, notes of kindness when I was going through a painful time. Robert Frost said that home is a place where, when you have to go there, they let you in. I would not have believed, a year ago, that Thurber was a place I would cheerfully call home. But I do!

Diminution

Mother shrank until she looked
like a tiny bisque doll,
her silver hair gone thin,
her blue china eyes filled
at the edges with tears.
Her world shrank, too,
only the morning sun
and a Mozart sonata to rest by.
She said she was settling
like an old house and it was true.
Slowly, slowly she imploded
like old structures do
when demolition crews raze them.
After the charges go off,
the buildings hang,
suspended by invisible strings,
before the walls all sag at once,
fall inward. Nothing left
but dust clouds
to darken the sunlit sky.
We scattered her ashes one April day,
watched them drift and swirl
over the aching green willows.

first published in *Living an August Life*, 1997

Possibly a Fling

a short story

Hours after the halls of Thurber Tower had quieted, Mabel sat at her living room window watching the city lights and listening to the quiet, steady drone of freeway traffic. Mabel was usually a good sleeper, but tonight she was troubled and sleep eluded her. She got up, put on her green chenille robe, poured a glass of brandy, and settled on her sofa "at the urban end."

Mabel and her husband, Carl, had moved to Thurber five years ago. Urged on by the children and unsettled by Carl's alarming incapacity to deal with even the most banal everyday tasks, the couple made the big move to a retirement community. They chose the one nearest to downtown, the symphony, museums, and the the big state university where Carl had been a classics professor for forty years.

Their marriage, like most, was satisfactory enough to keep them glued together for over fifty years. For the first thirty, it was her putting him through graduate school; the four children coming along in regular succession for eight years plus the twenty it took to raise them. If Mabel felt slighted in the bargain, she never let on but plunged into church work with a degree of ferocity that startled even her best friends.

Carl, on the other hand, spent more and more time on campus. Lunch at the Faculty Club and a highball after work with department colleagues guaranteed a late supper (and early bedtime) with Mabel often staying up late to read.

Nothing much changed except the ages of their children and grandchildren. Until Carl, only two years into retirement, began to fail. Thus the move to Thurber where life continued pretty much the same except for the addition of shuffleboard for her and the current affairs group for him. The same, that is, until Carl died suddenly of a ruptured aorta and took his well-disguised memory loss to the grave.

Now, it is three years later and Mabel has long since adjusted well to living alone. Her children are pleased that she has made many new friends, is reading more, joined a Book Club, and shows no outward signs of disintegrating in the near future. Mabel herself would report to anyone who asked that she was "quite happy."

Three months ago, Mabel accepted a new responsibility in the form of a two-year term on the Thurber Library Committees. Duties included book selection and library maintenance. Members made sure the library had current magazines on the table and potted plants on the window sill. Overdue books were discreetly retrieved and unwelcome dogs expelled with dispatch. One day, Mabel was shelving books. Unable to remember if Dos Passos went before or after Dostoevsky, she went to the unabridged dictionary (donated by a resident) to check.

When she looked up, she noticed a very tall, very white-haired man browsing in the back shelves. The height she noticed first because for fifty years she had slumped a bit when she was with Carl who had been distressingly short (as well as round.) The absolutely pure white hair of the library patron was an even more attractive feature for Mabel. Hers was an austere Ohio winter-gray and she had recently told a daughter she was going to have it tinted the color of fresh snow.

When the man turned around, she realized it was her new neighbor on the eighth floor, Roger Something-or-other, a widower from Bellefontaine. She had met him at the eighth-floor dinner the week before and had found him quite polite as well as charming. In addition, he played both bridge and canasta which was worth noting. Roger left the library after a few pleasantries and after checking out the new book, *The Hare With Amber Eyes* which she knew from the reviews to be a fairly ambitious read.

Mabel went about finishing her work at the library, stopped in the parlor for a short visit, and then to her apartment. She was unpleasantly irritable. Even Judy Woodruff set her teeth on edge when she reported on the continuing stalemate in the senate. Mabel thought Judy a bit too impartial when she blamed both parties for the current stalemate over the budget. Still at sixes and sevens, as her own mother had said when she was upset, Mabel went to bed with the current Elizabeth George mystery and read until the moon turned the corner on Thurber and she turned out the light.

Three weeks passed and Mabel continued to exchange pleasantries with Roger (as she did with all her neighbors.) They found themselves partners at the bridge table one night. She played well, drank too much wine, and went up the elevator with him at eleven o'clock. Then she saw him in the back pew of her very own First Congregational Church. She noticed his gray suit and maroon and gray tie. When the monthly wine and cheese get-together came round, she wore her favorite sweater and took an especially good cabernet to share.

Thus it went, until one day Mabel had to admit to herself that she had a crush on Roger. It was, in a word, embarrassing. Not only that, but silly and unbecoming for a grandmother about to be a "great." So instead of looking for Roger in all the gathering places, she took pains to avoid him and to direct her attention to her activities outside Thurber. One day, she was returning from the photography exhibit at the museum when she overheard the conversation in the parlor. "He's going to Florida for a week. He has a girlfriend in Palm Beach." "Oh my," another voice, "all that beautiful white hair to be ruffled up by someone else."

That night, Mabel sat at the window and sipped her brandy and watched the moon. Then she began to cry.

Delivering the Mail

Everyone has stories about waiting for the mail. At Boy Scout Camp or college or the forward lines in northern France. In small towns, getting the mail is still a social encounter as neighbors open their post office boxes while they chat with each other and the postmaster. So, too, at Thurber, where getting your mail is a pleasant way to descend in the byzantine elevators and engage for a few minutes with some of your friends. It is a call for Thurber dogs to appear for a biscuit. And, it is a way to take the temperature of the place, i.e., cheerful or dour, complaisant or excited.

For a few selected Thurber residents, the mail serves as a central organizing principle for every day but Sunday (or will it be Saturday and Sunday?). Waiting for the mail serves as a convenient reason for sitting in the front lounge for two hours each morning and for informing every resident who comes through the front door about the status of today's delivery. It is a social mechanism, a clock announcing lunchtime, as well as a convenient excuse for observing the latest *Sturm und Drang*.

Way less than half the residents use email so they still engage in the precocious and archaic habit of actually writing to each other, of experiencing the excitement of tearing open an anticipated invitation or deciphering the first cursive of a seven-year-old. In fact, some curious sociology student somewhere could write a dissertation on how email has reduced literacy and sociability simultaneously in planned communities.

Mail of another sort, in the form of announcements, appears every day under our doors. Paper usage is astounding! Yet it is a major artery for the delivery of the daily Thurber news. Today it is the new "chair yoga" schedule and a lecture by a well-known theologian. Tomorrow, who knows? You will just have to wait for the mail!

in my file marked funeral

it is not without reason to want
the last words, if only we knew

what, in the final word, matters;
what it is we most hope
our children will remember;
will tuck into drawers,
pull out when the dark times come;
words about how to catch life
in a butterfly net or sand in a sieve;
or put on walking boots
and put away childish things.

for these, for final words,
only poems I leave you.

WOODSHOP

DJW

Moving On

Next week, I will move to a slightly larger apartment on the fourth floor. The change means new, close-by neighbors; a quicker route to the outdoors by walking three flights (I know, I could have walked seven but I didn't); a closer-up view of a favorite sycamore tree (its bark looks like the skin of old people); and a new nook where I can read and write without bumping into my bed. Significant changes, I think to myself, but are they enough to keep me percolating?

Perhaps I will learn to draw, or use a lathe, or try an exercise class. The latter, I doubt. Why would I start seriously doing something I have never seriously liked doing?

Whatever . . . whatever . . .

Lord, let me stay excited.

CPSIA information can be obtained at www.ICGtesting.com
Printed in the USA
LVOW08s1435140714

394267LV00001B/11/P

9 780990 406136